Out of the Sea
Came Pirates!

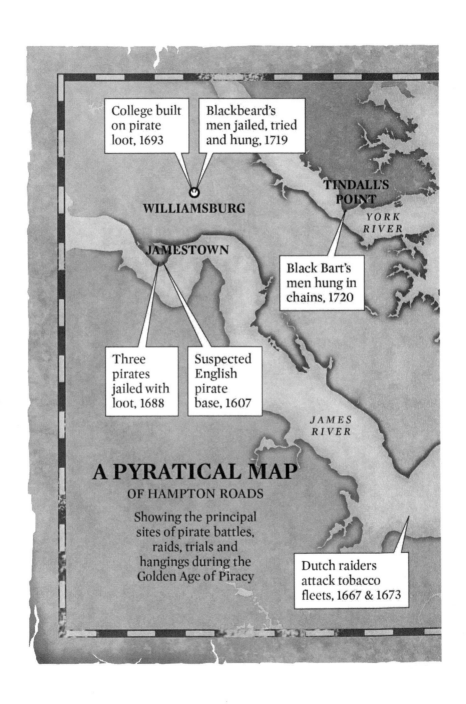

College built on pirate loot, 1693

Blackbeard's men jailed, tried and hung, 1719

TINDALL'S POINT

YORK RIVER

WILLIAMSBURG

JAMESTOWN

Black Bart's men hung in chains, 1720

Three pirates jailed with loot, 1688

Suspected English pirate base, 1607

JAMES RIVER

A PYRATICAL MAP
OF HAMPTON ROADS

Showing the principal sites of pirate battles, raids, trials and hangings during the Golden Age of Piracy

Dutch raiders attack tobacco fleets, 1667 & 1673

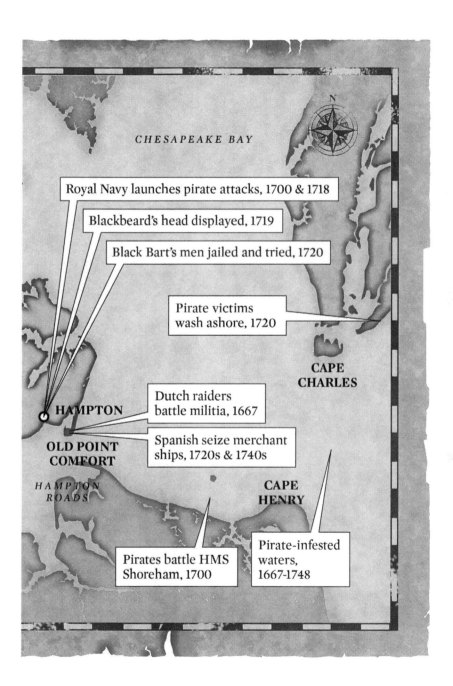

CHESAPEAKE BAY

N

Royal Navy launches pirate attacks, 1700 & 1718

Blackbeard's head displayed, 1719

Black Bart's men jailed and tried, 1720

Pirate victims
wash ashore, 1720

CAPE
CHARLES

Dutch raiders
battle militia, 1667

HAMPTON

Spanish seize merchant
ships, 1720s & 1740s

OLD POINT
COMFORT

HAMPTON
ROADS

CAPE
HENRY

Pirate-infested
waters,
1667-1748

Pirates battle HMS
Shoreham, 1700

Out of the Sea Came

PIRATES!

The Golden Age of Piracy in Hampton Roads

Mark St. John Erickson (signature)

Mark St. John Erickson

Daily Press Media Group

Out of the Sea Came Pirates!
The Golden Age of Piracy in Hampton Roads

Text copyright © 2012 by Mark St. John Erickson
dailypress.com

ISBN 978-0-9847121-2-0

10 9 8 7 6 5 4 3 2 1

Editing and design by Karen Morgan
Cover design by Wayne Elfman and Kevin Goyette

Daily Press Media Group
Digby Solomon, publisher
7505 Warwick Blvd.
Newport News, VA 23607
dailypress.com

Printed in the United States of America

For my little boy, Owen, who seldom walks with me along the old Hampton waterfront without asking about pirates.

Contents

Blackbeard the Pirate

Mark St. John Erickson

Out of the Sea Came Pirates!

Preface

This book began as a series of stories written for and published in the Daily Press in the spring of 2012 during the week leading up to the popular Blackbeard Pirate Festival in Hampton, Va.

Designed to look beyond the well-known connection between the old colonial port town and the infamous pirate's 1718 demise, it relies heavily on previous histories of piracy in and around the Chesapeake Bay, especially Donald G. Schomette's landmark 1985 book "Pirates of the Chesapeake: Being a True History of Pirates, Picaroons, and Raiders on Chesapeake Bay, 1610-1807" but also including such works as "Pirates of Colonial Virginia," which was published by Daily Press reporter Lloyd Haynes Williams in 1937. A 2008 book by North Carolina historian Kevin P. Duffus on "The Last Days of Black Beard the Pirate: Within Every Legend Lies a Grain of Truth" provided a compelling revisionist look at the fates of Blackbeard's crew, while North Carolina historian John Amrhein Jr.'s 2012 volume "Treasure Island: The Untold Story" added what appears to be a significant and previously unknown chapter to the region's colorful pirate history.

Many thanks are owed to Schomette, Duffus and Amrhein for their patience as they answered my questions and corrected my reading of their books in subsequent and often lengthy interviews. I also was fortunate to find similar authority and patience in a long series of interviews with Hampton Roads historians John V. Quarstein, Carson Hudson, J. Michael Cobb, Linda

Rowe, John Millar and Wilfred Kale — plus Mark G. Hanna of the University of California-San Diego — all of whom were uncommonly generous in sharing the fruits of their own curiosity and research. Additional thanks go to College of William and Mary archaeologist Joe B. Jones and Colonial Williamsburg historian Tom Hay for their insights into the trial and execution of Blackbeard's crew.

Thanks are also due to former Daily Press editor Mike Bambach, who greatly expanded the scope of this project, and Daily Press editor Karen Morgan, who read the results. Any errors are entirely my own, with far fewer appearing in print because of the efforts of everyone mentioned here.

Mark St. John Erickson

Out of the Sea Came Pirates!

Introduction

When your history reaches back as far as it does in Hampton Roads, the sheer passage of so much time gives you a lot of stories to tell — and many of the earliest and most colorful tales from the most historic part of the Virginia coast revolve around pirates.

Located just a few hours sail from the Gulf Stream and the sea lanes to Europe, the waters of the lower Chesapeake Bay were a busy international crossroads linking the rich tobacco, rice and sugar crops of Britain's American colonies with a constant stream of ships bearing cargoes across the Atlantic Ocean. And even before the first permanent English settlement was founded at Jamestown in 1607 by men who had earned notorious records as sea-going adventurers, Spanish galleons sailed past the mouth of the Bay carrying immense quantities of gold and silver from the seemingly inexhaustible mines of South America and Mexico.

That vast stream of wealth transformed the waters here into a prime hunting ground for pirates, privateers and sea raiders alike, ranging from English outcasts to French, Dutch and Spanish brigands over a period of more than 150 years. It also gave the busy port town of Hampton and the colonial capitals of Jamestown and Williamsburg an intimate and sometimes deadly connection to this predatory enterprise, whose practitioners knew Hampton Roads just as well for its jails, courts and gallows as its ship's stores, taverns and hiding places.

Just as striking as the riches that could be snatched from the local waters was the region's often unusually militant response to attacks from the sea. Stand-out pirate hunters such as Virginia Gov. Francis Nicholson went toe to toe with French pirates in a daylong battle off Lynnhaven Bay, while Lt. Gov. Alexander Spotswood not only hanged several accomplices of the notorious Black Bart but also organized the milestone naval expedition that killed Blackbeard and brought his head back to Hampton. So momentous were the Virginia colony's successes at imposing the rule of law on a renegade coast during the early 1700s that the change was felt all the way back to the West Indies and as far across the Atlantic as West Africa.

Indeed, despite the notoriety of the West Indies and the Caribbean, where pirates of various nationalities sailed out of Tortuga, Jamaica and the Bahamas for many years, Hampton Roads and the lower Chesapeake Bay played landmark roles in the golden age of piracy, overshadowing virtually every other part of what became the United States. No other body of water in North America was fought over so frequently — or produced so many tales about its long and often bloody links to the brigands of the sea. Here are some of those stories.

Out of the Sea Came Pirates!

Virginia goes on the hunt for Blackbeard

When news of one of history's most notorious pirate gatherings reached Virginia in late 1718, it couldn't have sparked more fear.

Just two days sail from Hampton Roads, the brutal Charles Vane and his second-in-command — Calico Jack Rackham — had joined the infamous Blackbeard in a week-long, rum-soaked cavort on Ocracoke Island in nearby North Carolina.

And so menacing was this apparent alliance and the specter of a buccaneer stronghold looming so close to home that it transformed the head of a colony long regarded as a choice piratical hunting ground into a determined pirate killer.

Lt. Gov. Alexander Spotswood knew all too well that — just one year before — the vital channel through Capes Henry and Charles had been closed for weeks by predatory sea rovers. Blackbeard himself had plundered nearly 50 ships in the Caribbean and Atlantic in only two years, and his notorious blockade of Charleston the previous spring made him an international villain.

Still, the secret expedition Spotswood organized in Williamsburg and Hampton finally eradicated this threat, leaving an indelible mark on the region.

Virginia became one of the most active combatants in the war against these brigands — and its triumph over the larger-than-life Blackbeard was a landmark blow that helped end the golden age of pirates.

"Like a lot of pirates, Blackbeard appeared out of nowhere after learning his trade as a privateer," historian John V. Quarstein says.

"In a very short time, he exploited his talents for daring, deviance and debauchery in ways that made him an emblem of piracy, and the battle in which he met his end has become one of history's most famous pirate battles."

Despite a persistent campaign against piracy, Virginia's geography combined with its rich tobacco fleets to turn the waters off the capes and the lower Chesapeake into a choice target.

Located near the northernmost reach of the Gulf Stream, the region was easily reached from as far away as the Caribbean, and the wealth of protected anchorages on its long coastline made it a haven for sea rovers intent on striking without being detected.

That's one reason why so many plied the waters here after the end of Queen Anne's War in 1713, when thousands of English privateers once employed against Spain and France turned to piracy. Even before ex-buccaneer Woodes Rogers became royal governor and drove them from the Bahamas in July 1718, they menaced Virginia and the East Coast in large numbers.

"Nobody paid any attention when they were raiding the Spanish," says maritime historian Donald G. Shomette, author of "Pirates on the Chesapeake Bay."

"But then it got out of hand."

No newly minted pirate stood out more than Blackbeard — aka Edward Teach or Thatch — who had shown courage and boldness as a privateer.

Tutored by the renowned Benjamin Hornigold, Blackbeard proved so adept at his new trade that he soon commanded an unusually large and well-armed ship of 40 guns and a fleet of smaller buccaneers. By the end of 1717, he had taken dozens of vessels, including a well-armed merchant ship that put up a lengthy battle.

That fearsome reputation and firepower panicked the port of Charleston when Blackbeard held it hostage in May 1718.

"This was a big tall man with long matted hair and a long black beard tied off in ribbons. So when he jumped on your deck armed with several braces of pistols as well as a sword, he was like a fury from hell," Quarstein says.

"His ship — the Queen Anne's Revenge — also was one of the most powerful pirate vessels and one of the most powerful ships in American waters at the time. So it's no surprise that Charleston and the whole East Coast were so fearful. Blackbeard captured and plundered every ship that passed by for a week, and he held some of the leading citizens for ransom."

Such daring and muscle might have enabled Blackbeard to defy two royal guardships roving the Chesapeake and spark similar panic in Hampton Roads.

But instead, he sailed to the Outer Banks, where he beached his ship, abandoned most of his crew and made his way inland to accept a royal pardon.

Within weeks, however, Blackbeard had returned to his piratical ways. And his notorious October rendezvous with Vane and Rackham sparked such alarm that Lt. Gov. Spotswood — citing a plea for help from North Carolina merchants — stealthily hired two light, fast sloops manned by Royal Navy seamen and sent them to Ocracoke Inlet on Nov. 17.

"This was all Spotswood's doing," Colonial Williamsburg

historian Linda Rowe says.

"And he was so afraid word might slip out that he kept it under wraps even from the Royal Council."

Armed with information from Blackbeard's former quartermaster, William Howard — who had been seized in Hampton earlier that year — Lt. Robert Maynard and his men located the pirate's hidden mooring on Nov. 21. The next morning they slipped through the shoals toward his ship, which greeted them with curses and cannon fire.

"Damnation seize my soul if I give you quarter or take any from you!" Blackbeard yelled, as he downed a bowl of liquor in a toast to his opponents.

Hoisting his black death's-head flag, the pirate swung his vessel into the hidden shallows and fired on his foes with simultaneous port and starboard broadsides. Nearly 30 Englishmen fell in the deadly barrage, after which all three ships ran aground.

Struggling to free his sloop, Maynard hurried to close with the pirate before another broadside could do him in. He then told his men to wait below deck with pistols and cutlasses ready.

Pirate grenades filled the air with smoke and confusion as Blackbeard pulled alongside, yelling "Let's jump aboard and cut them to pieces!" But as the brigands lept aboard, Maynard's men rushed out in a fierce hand-to-hand melee.

Breaking Maynard's sword, Blackbeard was stepping in for the kill when he was struck in the neck and throat from behind. Blood splattered as he continued to fight, then fell to the deck after being stabbed and shot from all sides.

"He lived up to his legend fully," Quarstein says.

"He took six pistol shots and more than 20 sword wounds before he died — and he was cocking a pistol as he dropped."

Not until Jan. 3 — after rounding up Blackbeard's accomplices in North Carolina — did Maynard return to Hampton with the

Out of the Sea Came Pirates!

severed head of the pirate swinging from his bowsprit.

Cheers and cannon fire saluted this grisly arrival, and the celebration in Williamsburg five days later was just as emphatic.

"Blackbeard was Public Enemy No. 1 — and now Spotswood had his head," Quarstein says.

"So this was a big deal."

The gallows where
Blackbeard's crew swung

When Lt. Robert Maynard sailed back into Hampton, Va., on Jan. 3, 1719, the grisly sight of Blackbeard's severed head swinging from his bowsprit marked the end of one of history's most notorious pirates.

But for nine of the crewmen who fought alongside Blackbeard — and six other accomplices seized with his loot in Bath, N.C. — the landing at the King Street docks was merely the opening of a new and — for some, at least — ultimately fatal chapter.

Taken to Williamsburg to stand trial, they were held in the 1704 public "gaol" on Nicholson Street just north of the Capitol. At least some faced an admiralty court on March 12, when — according to the most cited source — one was acquitted, one pardoned and the rest sentenced to hang.

No direct records of that trial or the execution survive. But in 1992, archaeologists from the College of William and Mary discovered the remains of a large, triangular gallows one mile from the gaol and just yards from Capitol Landing Road.

With its distinctive shape, the early 1700s scaffold was clearly modeled after the infamous "Triple Tree" gallows at Tyburn, London, archaeologist Joe B. Jones says. And with each leg

Out of the Sea Came Pirates!

measuring 11 feet long, it also boasted the size needed to carry out a mass hanging.

"This was designed to handle more than one person at a time," Jones says.

"And it was big enough to allow the simultaneous execution of the 13 members of Blackbeard's crew."

If the sentence was carried out as many historians believe, the site on what was then called Gallows Road was an easily accessible and highly visible location.

Dense scatters of early 1700s artifacts have been found around the postholes from which the gallows rose, including coins suggesting that some onlookers placed bets on the death throes of the condemned.

"In London, people turned out in large crowds for the execution of notorious criminals," says Tom Hay, site supervisor of the courthouse and Capitol in Colonial Williamsburg.

"And it's overwhelmingly likely that it happened here for the execution of Blackbeard's crew."

Still, according to the log of HMS Pearl — whose sailors took part in the Nov. 22, 1718 battle that killed Blackbeard — two condemned pirates were taken from the ship and hung on Jan. 28, 1719 in Hampton.

In Bath, N.C. — where Blackbeard and some of his crew lived for part of 1718 — surviving property and court records suggest that four of the men were still alive long after they were reported hanged.

Lt. Gov. Alexander Spotswood's discussion of pirate testimony in a letter dated before the March 12 trial suggests some previous legal proceeding took place — perhaps one that invoked a December 1718 royal pardon offering amnesty to repentant pirates.

North Carolina historian Kevin P. Duffus — author of "The

Last Days of Blackbeard the Pirate" — believes only six members of the pirate crew died on the gallows because of the king's mercy. He also thinks all six hangings were carried out in Hampton.

That may explain an unusual burial discovered in the 1980s by archaeologists probing what was once called Customhouse Point.

Laid face down between the low- and high-water marks, the orientation of the remains reflected a common ritual for the interment of supposedly "soul-less" buccaneers.

"It's exactly how they buried the pirates hanged in Charlestown the year before," Duffus says.

Likely hung in chains after their deaths, the remains of the pirates may have been displayed as a grisly warning to others.

Blackbeard's head is said to have been mounted on a pike and placed on the banks of the Hampton River for the same reason.

"Plenty of people have written about it. It was the sort of thing that would have been done — and we have pretty good evidence from the piece of land that's always been called 'Blackbeard's Point,'" says Hampton History Museum Curator J. Michael Cobb.

"But whether it actually happened is a whole other matter — because there's no mention of it in the log of the Pearl."

Dutch raiders prowl Hampton Roads

Of all the sea raiders who preyed on Hampton Roads, none wreaked more havoc or spawned more fear than the Dutch.

During the Anglo-Dutch wars, especially — when investors in what was then the world's most powerful maritime nation plowed millions of guilders into outfitting privateers — the sight of the tricolored Dutch flag flying over their fast, well-armed ships sent the region into a frenzy.

Twice these Dutch "kapers" prowled Hampton Roads like wolves among sheep, panicking the hapless tobacco fleet and bloodying the roving militia companies attempting to protect the shores.

And when they sailed off with their loot of Virginia Bright-leaf, they left a wake of burned hulls, dead defenders and frayed nerves stretching from Old Point Comfort to Jamestown.

"The Dutch were incredibly accomplished raiders. They were a sea-faring nation with some heavy-hitting sailors who had beaten the English navy time and time again," says maritime historian Donald G. Shomette, author of "Raid on America: The Dutch Naval Campaign of 1672-1674."

Mark St. John Erickson   15

"So when the kapers came into the Chesapeake, people had good reason to fear them. They were more dreaded than the Spanish."

Led by commander Abraham Crijnssen, four warships from the province of Zeeland — which was the Dutch republic's most ardent hotbed of privateering — sailed past the Virginia capes on June 1, 1667, after wresting the colony of Surinam from the English.

They entered Hampton Roads four days later, hoisting English colors and calling out their soundings in English in order to disguise their approach from the old and leaky guardship Elizabeth, which was laid up after crossing the Atlantic just the month before, and a fleet of 20 merchantmen laden with tobacco.

Firing three quick broadsides of hot shot into the guardship's hull, the freebooters snapped up the stunned tobacco ships, then began sending out landing parties in search of water, provisions and plunder.

Roving militiamen repelled them at every turn, but not without sustaining such casualties as royal councilor Col. Miles Cary of Warwick County, who was mortally wounded on June 10 while defending the run-down, poorly armed fort at Old Point.

Frantically attempting to mount a defense, Gov. William Berkeley ordered 900 militiamen to board nine armed merchantmen anchored on the York River and 300 others to man three more ships on the James.

But he was still trying to convince his reluctant force to sail downriver in a two-pronged counterattack when the Dutch — who had taken more prizes than they could man — burned many of the tobacco ships and sailed away with the others.

"By far the most damage done here during the age of piracy was done by the Dutch," Williamsburg historian Carson Hudson says.

"They knew they could hurt us by attacking the tobacco fleet, and this wouldn't be the last time they came to hunt in the Chesapeake."

Three years later, six well-armed kapers from Zeeland joined three others from Amsterdam to follow up on Crijnssen's success, which had earned him both a fortune and a medal.

Led by the daring 31-year-old Cornelis Evertsen, who was known as "Kees the Devil," and veteran commander Jacob Binckes, the expedition sailed into the bay on July 10, 1673, after carrying out a series of Caribbean raids financed by the Dutch West Indies Company.

"This is the biggest and most powerful fleet in the West Hemisphere," Shomette says, "and its target is the great tobacco fleet."

This time, however, Virginia's defenders didn't fall for the ruse when the Dutch approached Hampton Roads flying St. George's Cross and hailing passing vessels in English.

Instead, they sent 40 tobacco ships fleeing upriver, then tried to buy time by blocking the Dutch with two Royal Navy frigates and 11 armed merchantmen.

The squadron had just nosed out of the James when an unsuspecting flotilla of 8 Maryland tobacco ships emerged from the upper bay. So part of the English force broke away in an attempt to get between them and the Dutch raiders.

Drawing within a quarter mile of their foes, the English then turned back toward the James, sparking an uneven running battle across Hampton Roads as they dodged their pursuers. All six armed merchantmen ran aground as they fled, leaving the two Royal Navy ships to fend off the superior Dutch fleet.

Still, one English warship tacked across their path and engaged Evertsen and his 44-gun flagship for an hour, during which "all his greate maste and his fore topmast (were) desperately wounded, and most of his rigging shot." Then the out-gunned vessel came about, choking off the Dutchman's wind to earn an unexpected escape into the Elizabeth River.

Despite this loss, the privateers had little problem picking off the armed merchantmen that had grounded, and the next morning they began pursuing at least 34 tobacco ships fleeing upriver. Only contrary winds and dangerous shoals kept them at bay, stranding two Dutch vessels while a dozen fat merchant ships fled into the safety of the Nansemond River and 20 more scurried up the James.

Anchoring his biggest ships to protect his trapped comrades, Evertsen sent his smallest, lightest vessels upriver, where they burned numerous grounded merchantmen and captured several others.

He continued this game of cat-and-mouse for days, halting only after the passengers of a captured New York ship reported that the former Dutch colony was virtually defenseless.

By the time he and Binckes sailed out on July 22 to retake New York, the Dutch fleet had captured or torched most of the great tobacco fleet and seized or destroyed thousands of hogsheads of the golden weed with few losses.

They'd also thrown Virginia into a state of panic.

"It was the largest and most destructive attack of its kind," Hampton History Museum curator J. Michael Cobb says.

"No one else did anything on a scale like this."

William and Mary built on pirate loot

Few universities can look back on a history so venerable as the College of William and Mary in the colonial capitol of Williamsburg, Va.

Chartered by royal decree in 1693, America's second oldest college soon became home to its first law school and went on to educate so many Founding Fathers that it's been called the "Alma Mater of a Nation."

Less well known, however, is its link to pirate loot.

Sailing from the nearby town of Hampton and the Eastern Shore more than a decade earlier, buccaneers Lionel Wafer, John Hinson and Edward Davis spent five years pillaging and exploring the distant west coast of South America, compiling a record of plunder and adventure that few other sea rovers equaled.

And rarely did any face down the tangle of legal threats that ensnared them — then raised the specter of the noose — after they were arrested with their pirate swag in 1688 while trying to retire in Hampton Roads.

"This was a huge amount of treasure — a king's ransom — and everybody was trying to get a piece of it," says historian Donald G. Shomette, author of "Pirates on the Chesapeake."

Mark St. John Erickson

"But it was William and Mary's founder — the Rev. James Blair — who connected with them, and who traded his help for part of the school's endowment."

This curious case of piratical philanthropy reaches back to 1682, when a band of daring Englishmen bought the ship Revenge and hired its previous captain — a veteran freebooter named John Cooke — with the intention of making their fortunes as sea raiders.

Cooke quickly sailed to Panama, where he tempered his amateur crew through the addition of Wafer — who had previously been his ship's surgeon — and the experienced Hinson. Then he set course for Virginia, where he careened his vessel for repairs on the Eastern Shore while looking up two other old shipmates in the tough seafaring town of Hampton.

William Dampier had already sailed around the world, and like Wafer, he would later publish his memoirs, penning amazing accounts of exploration and adventure that would later influence Jonathan Swift, author of "Gulliver's Travels" and Daniel Defoe, author of "Robinson Crusoe," as well as naturalist Charles Darwin.

Davis would eventually be hanged for consorting with the notorious Capt. William Kidd, but not before he took Cooke's place and led pioneering voyages to Easter Island, the Galapagos, New Zealand and possibly Antarctica.

"This was like the Wild West," Shomette says.

"Everybody was out for adventure."

Plunder was a driving factor, too, and — after winning a formidable new ship named the Bachelor's Delight in a West African card game — the crew sailed across the South Atlantic and rounded Cape Horn.

There they launched a five-year campaign of piracy in which they seized ships, ransomed captives and sacked towns, leaving

Out of the Sea Came Pirates!

a trail of terror that stretched from Chile to Panama.

By 1687, their vessel was the flagship of a dangerous buccaneer fleet that could muster 1,000 men and strike unsuspecting targets deep inland. But with their coffers full, the crew finally turned back through the Straits of Magellan and sailed north, intent on finding places to retire.

Booking passage from the West Indies to Philadelphia, the pirate trio and Davis' slave had already made their way down the Chesapeake Bay when they were arrested near Old Point Comfort on June 22, 1688 with three chests heavily laden with pieces of eight and silver plate.

"These guys weren't stupid. They were trying to come into Hampton Roads through the back door," Shomette says.

"But they couldn't get past the guardship at the mouth of the bay."

Thrown into irons at Jamestown, the trio pretended to be traders but were fingered by the slave.

Then they tried to claim amnesty under a 1687 proclamation issued by the recently deposed King James II, only to be denied by Gov. Francis Howard, who wrote back to the new government of King William III asking for its decision.

Ultimately, the hapless captives were released and instructed to return to England for the pardon. But their treasure was ensnared in legal limbo, with everyone from the captain of the royal guardship to Sir Robert Holmes — the unscrupulous head of the crown's anti-piracy campaign — trying to fill their own pockets.

Shrewdly, the pirates stalled at Jamestown to watch over their imperiled loot, and they persistently laid claim to the cache despite their increasingly impoverished condition. They also filed petition after petition in Virginia and London, where they enlisted the influence of wealthy merchant Micajah Perry.

Not until they met Rev. Blair in London, however, did piracy and piety unite in the legal loophole that freed their loot and gave the crown cover for its decision.

"I do humbly certify," Blair wrote on Feb. 18, 1691, "that the Petitioners have devoted and secured towards the carrying on the pious design of a free School and College in Virginia, the Summe of three hundred pounds, providing that the order be given for restoring to them their money."

"Blair was an opportunist. He needed the money desperately — and he may well have contacted them after arriving in London," says Wilford Kale, author of the William and Mary history "Hark Upon the Gale."

"Pirate loot may not have been part of the puzzle to begin with, but it became a very important part in the end, and he used whatever influence he had to get what he could for the college's endowment."

Still, two years passed before Blair returned to Virginia with his charter.

There he quickly found use for a sum that today would be worth — depending on the formula used — from $900,000 to $9 million.

"In those days 300 pounds was a boatload of money," Kale says.

"I can see it going right into the Wren Building."

Out of the Sea Came Pirates!

Governor goes
toe to toe with pirates

Gov. Francis Nicholson was nothing if not a man of action.

Long before coming to Virginia in 1698, he'd shown his mettle time and time again, fighting Moors in North Africa, English rebels at the battle of Sedgemoor and hostile Indians in New York and New England.

Still, no one would have raised an eyebrow had he hesitated on the afternoon of April 28, 1700, when a Royal Navy officer interrupted him at a prominent Hampton home with news of pirates. Even the other navy captain in the room — who'd stopped to pay his respects — had no doubts about leaving the protesting governor behind as he rushed to the King Street docks and readied his ship for battle.

By 10 p.m, however, Nicholson had not only alerted the militia on the south side of the James but made his way across the dark waters in a rowboat to board the HMS Shoreham.

By 7 a.m. the next day, he was standing on the Shoreham's quarterdeck, firing his pistols at close range in a bloody, 10-hour clash that defined him as one of the era's great pirate hunters.

"I can't think of any other battle like it," says Mark G. Hanna, a University of California-San Diego historian who studied co-

Mark St. John Erickson

lonial piracy at the College of William and Mary's Omohundro Institute of Early American History and Culture.

"Nicholson went toe to toe with the pirates — and ended up being a huge story in London. He was a hero."

Nicholson's daring and resolve may have been borne of frustration.

Just nine months earlier, the small, inadequately armed HMS Essex Prize had been outgunned and outsailed in a humiliating Chesapeake Bay clash with a pirate pretending to be the dreaded Capt. William Kidd.

And while the newly arrived Shoreham — with its 32 guns — introduced a larger, far more potent warship as the sentinel of the Chesapeake, Capt. William Passenger had been forced to make do with a short-handed crew weakened still more by inexperienced and underage sailors.

Still, the captives scooped up by French pirate Louis Guittar as he bore down on the Virginia capes from the West Indies knew nothing about this recent change of guard.

Not until his ship had overwhelmed eight rich merchant vessels — including one carrying an intoxicating cargo of strong beer and red wine — did a tortured carpenter finally reveal the potential challenge waiting on the other side of Hampton Roads.

Emboldened by their successes and the alcohol, however, Guittar and the 150-man crew of the 20-gun La Paix scoffed at the threat and focused instead on plundering the small fleet of prizes they'd anchored off Lynnhaven Inlet.

They were still groggy from drink when the Shoreham sent a shot across their bow just after dawn, setting the stage for what would become a murderous battle.

"It was a tough, close fight with severe casualties. Peter Heyman — the Hampton customs collector — was killed by a volley from the La Paix as he stood next to Nicholson firing from the

Shoreham's deck," Colonial Williamsburg historian Carson Hudson says.

"At times, they were blasting away at each other from pistol range — only 20 to 30 yards — and the pirate ship was shot to pieces."

Knowing they would be hanged if taken, Guittar and his crew fought for their lives, firing broadside after broadside as they attempted to maneuver in and board their outnumbered foe for a more favorable fight at close quarters.

But time after time, Passenger rallied his crew of boys in a heroic display of courage and seamanship, maintaining his distance and his advantage on the windward side of the clash even as his short-handed gunners struggled to answer the pirates' volleys.

Spectators watched from the shore as the grisly fight wore on, felling so many pirates they clogged the decks and had to be thrown overboard. Others looked on from Old Point Comfort as the Shoreham's mainmast fell in the thunderous cannon fire and gunpowder smoke filled the approach to Hampton Roads.

Not until late afternoon did the Royal Navy's slow but superior fire finally prevail. Consuming nearly 30 barrels of powder, its guns fired 1,671 rounds in a determined attack that "shot all his masts, yards, sailes, rigging all to shatters, unmounted several guns and hull almost beaten to pieces," an observer reported.

The end came soon after the Shoreham's guns blasted the La Paix's rudder, leaving the floating wreck helplessly grounded. But as the pirates lowered their blood-red flag, their captain played one last gambit.

Priming 30 barrels of explosives with a trail of gunpowder, Guittar vowed to blow up his ship and 50 captives if not given quarter. Nicholson replied with the pirates' threats of "Broil! Broil! Broil!" ringing in his ears, scrawling a note that promised to "referr him and his men to the mercy of my Royal Master

King William the third ..."

Of the 124 buccaneers who surrendered, 111 were manacled and transported from Hampton to London, where they were tried and condemned to death.

Three others were convicted in an admiralty court at Hampton and hanged on the beaches overlooking the scene of the battle.

Customs officer Peter Heyman was buried in the yard at Hampton's third St. John's Church, where his grave is marked by a stone Nicholson commissioned.

"(He) went voluntarily aboard ye king's Shippe Shoreham in pursuit of a pyrate who greatly infested this coast," it reads.

"After he had behaved himself seven hours with undaunted courage (he) was killed with small shot ...(as) he stood next ye Govenour upon the quarter deck ..."

Black Bart vows to avenge hangings

Bartholomew Roberts didn't start out wanting to be a pirate.

But not for nothing did the Welshman captured by a bucca-neer crew in 1719 get the nickname "Black Bart" — or compile a record of plunder that ranks among history's greatest.

In just three years, the daring brigand took 470 prizes, includ-ing an extraordinary Brazilian treasure ship plucked from a fleet guarded by two powerful men-of-war. He roved from West Af-rica and the West Indies to Newfoundland, where 22 ships gave up without a shot in one of the Golden Age of Piracy's most celebrated feats of boldness and intimidation.

Capable, outspoken and flamboyant, the Crimson Pirate embraced a strict code of allegiance, too, exacting an often cruel revenge when any shipmate was harmed or taken.

That's why in 1720 — after six of his crew members had been seized in Hampton, tried and hanged, then trussed up in chains as a warning — his vow of vengeance threw the whole country-side from Old Point Comfort to Williamsburg into an uproar.

"When Black Bart said he was going to get you, he got you," historian John Quarstein says, describing the power of Roberts' fleet and his bent for settling scores.

Mark St. John Erickson

"And when he got the governor of Martinique, he hung him from the yardarm of his own ship."

Roberts and his crew became the stuff of pirate legend when they sailed alone into the capital of Brazil, captured the richest of 42 treasure ships and eluded two powerful 72-gun guardships with ease.

Their phenomenal haul included 40,000 Portuguese gold coins worth at least $9 million today and a fortune in gems, sugar, tobacco and hides. They also captured a cache of jewelry made for Portugal's nobility, the richest of which was a diamond-studded cross intended for the king.

Fleeing to the infamous pirate refuge at Devil's Island, the crew soon parted ways, with most sailing to the West Indies under one of Roberts' lieutenants. There they meandered, relieving various ships of their goods until stopping the Virginia-bound West River Merchant.

Eager to retire with their loot, eight buccaneers coerced the vessel's captain into providing passage to the Chesapeake Bay. They reached the Virginia Capes in February 1720, with one band of pirates coming ashore on Hampton's Back River and another landing in the town itself.

"As soon as they came ashore their first care was to find a Tavern, where they might ease themselves of their Golden Luggage," the American Weekly Mercury in Philadelphia reported.

"For some time they lived very profusely treating all that came into their Company, and there being in the House English Women Servants, who had the good fortune by some Hidden Charms, to appear pleasing to these Picaroons, they set them Free, giving their Master 30 pounds."

With their new "wives" in tow, the freebooters lived lavishly, laying down hard cash in a region that seldom saw any other payment than tobacco. So within days they were jailed by Lt.

Out of the Sea Came Pirates!

Gov. Alexander Spotswood in Elizabeth City County as suspected pirates.

"In places like Charleston and Newport, all kinds of pirates are coming back from sea and settling into society with very little resistance," says Mark G. Hanna, a University of California-San Diego historian who studied colonial piracy at the College of William and Mary's Omohundro Institute of Early American History and Culture.

"But when they come to Virginia, they're being hunted down and arrested very quickly. Any pirate who came to the Chesapeake to retire soon found out they'd made a mistake."

Tried in Hampton, the sea rovers claimed they had been forced into piracy. But two Portuguese captives forced to sail with them on the West River Merchant testified to their crimes.

The captain of the coerced vessel gave damning evidence, too, prompting the doomed yet defiant pirates to curse their accusers.

"Six of them appeared the most profligate Wretches I ever heard of," Spotswood later wrote.

"And (they) vow'd if they were again at liberty they would spare none alive that should fall into the hands."

So brazen were the condemned that one drank a final glass of wine at the gallows, toasting, "Damnation to the Governor and Confusion to the Colony."

Spotswood responded by taking the bodies of the four worst from the scaffolds at Urbanna and Tindall's Point and hanging them in chains.

That grisly insult was answered a few months later by a message of vengeance carried by a terrified merchant captain. Black Bart had vowed to teach Virginia a lesson and — with the expected addition of another ship — his fleet could bring 112 guns to do it.

Rattled by this dire threat, the colony raced to build a series of watch stations, warning beacons and gun batteries stretching from Cape Henry, Old Point Comfort and Gloucester to the Rappahannock River.

But when news came that Roberts had beaten a powerful French warship and hanged the governor of Martinique found on board, the state of panic only grew.

History didn't record Spotswood's response when, in early 1722, he learned that the dreaded pirate had been killed in battle off West Africa.

But in 1724 he refused to sail to England in anything less than a man of war.

"If those barbarous Wretches can be moved to cut off the Nose & Ears of a Master for but correcting his own Sailors, what inhuman treatment must I expect, should I fall within their power," he asked.

"(I) have been markt as the principle object of their vengeance, for cutting off their arch Pirate Thatch, with all his grand Designs, & making so many of their Fraternity to swing in the open air of Virginia."

Spanish raiders
infest local waters

Glance through American newspapers from 1720 to 1748 and one change becomes abundantly clear.

The scourge of English pirates that had darkened shipping reports since the century began was replaced almost overnight by a new menace — this time an infestation of Spanish privateers swarming up from St. Augustine and Havana.

No place attracted the Don Benitos and Don Pedros of this predatory fleet more than the waters off the Virginia Capes and the Chesapeake Bay.

Countless times they slipped into Hampton Roads to hunt for unwary targets, taking ship after ship from such seemingly safe harbors as Old Point Comfort near the mouth of the Hampton River.

"Whenever Spain went to war with England — which was often — it went to war with Virginia," Colonial Williamsburg historian Carson Hudson says.

"That's when these privateers would sail up the Gulf Stream to the Capes and into Hampton Roads."

Virginia Lt. Gov. Alexander Spotswood was still celebrating his 1718 triumph over the notorious Blackbeard — and the recent hanging of six members of Bartholomew "Black Bart" Roberts' crew — when the first sign of the new Spanish plague appeared off the Capes on April 28, 1720.

Within days, this privateer sloop of 4 guns and 70 men was followed by more sea rovers from St. Augustine, including one so bold it chased its prey into Hampton Roads and made the panicked ships of the colony's merchant fleet scatter.

"Almost overnight word of Spanish privateering attacks up and down the Atlantic seaboard began to filter into the seaports," says maritime historian Donald G. Shomette, author of "Pirates on the Chesapeake."

"The Chesapeake was especially vulnerable because you could ride the Gulf Stream all the way from St. Augustine to Cape Hatteras. It took just a week-and-a-half to get here."

Some of the damage the Spanish inflicted can be seen in a July 1720 report describing the plight of 70 English seamen who were captured and put ashore on the York River.

Other victims were far less fortunate, including 18 whose remains washed up on the Eastern Shore.

"Some of them (were) tied back to back," the American Weekly Mercury of Philadelphia reported.

"One a Gentleman ... was found with his hands tied behind him, and his two great toes tied together."

Adding to this terror was the fact that the latest war with Spain had ended.

Its sea-borne campaign of plunder and fear didn't stop, however, until a well-armed Virginia sloop manned by 60 Royal Navy seaman sailed under a white flag to St. Augustine, where it confronted the governor with a royal proclamation confirming the halt of hostilities — then demanded restitution.

Despite the subsequent pause in attacks, Spotswood wrote angrily to the Lords Commissioners of Trade and Foreign Plantations, complaining about the Royal Navy vessel that was too old and leaky to protect the colony's shipping.

He also insisted that Virginia's merchantmen would never be safe as long as the Spanish ruled St. Augustine.

"When they did send Royal Navy vessels to defend the Bay, they were almost invariably old and ready to sink when they got here," Shomette says.

"So the Spanish had a pretty open season. There was nothing to stop them."

A second wave of attacks took place in 1724 when Spanish privateer Don Benito sailed to the Chesapeake aboard a "Guardia de la Costa" vessel outfitted, armed and commissioned by the governor of Cuba.

Soon after making the Capes, he chased down the Hampton merchantman "John and Mary," yelling "God damn you, strike, you English doggs, strike!" as the hapless crew scurried to heave to and haul down their colors.

Then he stripped it of 76 slaves, a cache of gold dust, various weapons and about 400 gallons of rum before seizing two more ships and sailing away unmolested.

Two decades of peace passed before the Spanish carried out their third and worst series of raids with not even a leaky old guardship to oppose them.

They seized dozens and dozens of vessels between 1741 and '45, when Spanish privateer Don Pedro arrived with a 36-gun ship and five-vessel fleet that left the entire East Coast gasping.

So pestilent was the threat that insurance rates for outbound vessels rose from a peacetime norm of 3 or 4 percent to nearly 25 percent, Shomette says. By that fall, London brokers were refusing to insure any ships headed for the Chesapeake — and those in Bristol were demanding premiums equal to nearly half the value of the cargoes.

Mark St. John Erickson

Not until two 44-gun guardships began patrolling the Virginia Station in 1748 did the predators who had roved past Old Point Comfort finally begin to back off.

By summer's end, the determined commanders had taken so many Spanish privateers that they sent a small fleet of captured ships back to Havana in exchange for English prisoners of war.

"It's remarkable how long it took London to commit Royal Navy ships that were actually capable of defending the Virginia Capes and the Chesapeake Bay," says Mark G. Hanna, a University of California-San Diego historian who studied colonial piracy at the College of William and Mary's Omohundro Institute of Early American History and Culture.

"But when you have an empire to build and so many powerful enemies to contend with, the idea of taking a man of war away from your fleet and sending it to Virginia probably ranks no higher than number 50 on your to-do list."

Out of the Sea Came Pirates!

Jamestown's English colonists strike fear in Spanish hearts

As much as English colonists feared the Spanish privateers who infested Virginia's coast during the 1720s and '40s, the Spanish feared the English just as much.

For nearly two centuries before these raids, English privateers had attacked Spain and its colonial possessions with an opportunistic passion. And Spain's forays into the Chesapeake Bay during the 1700s gave it the chance to strike back at a settlement it had loathed since the birth of Jamestown in 1607.

As far as King Phillip III and his ambassador to England had been concerned, that struggling outpost was nothing more than a nest of sea bandits poised to strike Spain's American colonies and Gulf Stream shipping lanes from a prime location.

"When the Spanish looked at the people behind the settlement, all they could see were pirates," says historian James Horn, vice president of research and historical interpretation at Colonial Williamsburg.

Mark St. John Erickson

"And they were right."

Among the most prominent leaders of the 1607 expedition that founded Jamestown was Christopher Newport, who had not only sailed with the English privateer Sir Francis Drake against Spanish holdings in the West Indies but also helped defeat the Spanish Armada in 1588.

Newport later lost one of his arms attacking a Spanish vessel off the coast of Cuba and — as the Spanish well knew — his capture of the Portuguese treasure ship Madre de Deus off the Azores in 1592 represented the richest prize taken by a Englishman in the 1500s, Horn says.

Virginia Company co-founder and Jamestown co-commander Bartholomew Gosnold had been a notable privateer, too, seizing Spanish prizes worth a fortune.

His friends and co-investors in the Virginia colony included such figures as wealthy London merchant Sir Thomas Smythe, the Earls of Warwick and Southampton and Lord de la Warr — all of whom had spent and made considerable sums of money outfitting privateers.

Warwick and de la Warr, in particular, were co-owners along with Virginia deputy governor Samuel Argall of the privateer vessel "Treasurer," which took part in the historic expedition that brought the first known Africans to Old Point Comfort after capturing a Portuguese slave ship in 1619.

So strong were the colony's links to privateering that two letters donated to Colonial Williamsburg in 2011 document an exchange between King Philip III and the Duke of Medina Sidonia — the former commander of the Armada — and illustrate their fears about the piratical potential of the infant settlement at Jamestown.

Other correspondence by such figures as Don Diego de Molina — who was held captive at Jamestown in 1611 — echo their suspicions and argue that the colony should be destroyed.

"(Jamestown is) a hydra in its infancy," Molina wrote. "The advantages of this place make it very suitable for a gathering of all the pirates in Europe."

The heist that inspired "Treasure Island"

In the 262 years since he last sailed from the King Street docks, Hampton merchant captain Owen Lloyd has been forgotten.

Long gone are any memories of the house he owned on Queen Street near St. John's Church — or his voyages carrying peas, corn and barrel-making supplies to the West Indies to trade for sugar, rum and molasses.

Yet hidden in archives around the Atlantic, Lloyd left a trail of records that not only describe his up-and-down fortunes as a Virginia mariner but also his exploits as a privateer — then as a leader in one of the greatest pirate heists ever recorded.

So sensational was his 1750 escape from Ocracoke with 52 chests of Spanish silver that newspapers and governments in five countries followed his trail. And when Lloyd stopped to bury his loot on a deserted Virgin Islands beach, he planted the seeds of an adventure story that — 133 years later — may have inspired the pioneering pirate novel, "Treasure Island."

"In the beginning, Owen Lloyd was just a name that kept cropping up. But nobody really knew who he was," says North Carolina author, diver and historian John Amrhein Jr., who first took note of the Hampton sailor in 1978 while searching for the wreck of the Spanish ship La Galga on the Eastern Shore.

"But the more I looked into it, the more I found, and the more I wanted to know. This was a guy who pulled off the equivalent of a $10 million to $20 million heist that — financially, at least — outstripped anything Blackbeard ever did."

Since then, Amrhein has pieced together a fat file of records ranging from property logs in Hampton and Norfolk to naval and legal archives in England, Spain, Denmark, the Netherlands and the West Indies.

His sources include deeds, shipping returns, admiralty papers and official reports as well as expense accounts, newspapers and — in one revealing instance — a plaintive letter written by Lloyd from a Norfolk jail after the loss of his ship to Spanish privateers all but bankrupted his business.

Using hired researchers and translators to help, the former medical insurance auditor turned Outer Banks real estate man has breathed new life into a biography that was blank.

"Every place I went I struck gold," Amrhein says.

"But outside of war, there aren't many things as well-documented as crimes like this, and it was notorious."

Amrhein traced Lloyd back to his birth in Wales and his early years as a Royal Navy midshipman.

At age 20, he left the service to work as a merchant sailor, soon becoming master of a 60-ton, 8-gun sloop that traded from St. Kitts in the West Indies to Ocracoke, Hampton Roads and Boston.

Lloyd was sailing off Martinique in 1745 when — during a time of war with France — he seized a French Guineaman loaded with slaves, gold dust and elephant tusks. So rich was his share that he bought his ship and moved with his wife-to-be to Norfolk.

There he joined his older brother John, who became master of the company's ship after Owen agreed to captain a vessel to the West Indies for Norfolk merchant and former mayor John Hutchings. But when the Lloyds removed the guns from their sloop at the insistence of Hampton merchant Alexander MacKenzie, who wanted more room for a cargo of Madeira wine, their rising star ran into trouble.

The elder Lloyd had almost returned from Portugal when he was captured off Cape Henry by a Spanish privateer. That forced his brother to mortgage everything he owned — including 24 slaves — and sail to Havana with the ransom.

The disastrous reversal left Owen hustling even after his move to Hampton, where he roamed the waterfront taverns looking for jobs. But after nearly three years of erratic work — and a run-in off the Capes with another Spaniard — Lloyd left for St. Kitts to start over.

His vessel was nearing the Outer Banks when it began leaking in the aftermath of a violent hurricane. The same storm brought a dismasted Spanish treasure ship into Ocracoke, too, where Lloyd was not only hired to pilot the vessel in but also found a place aboard one of two sloops chartered to transfer its cargo to Norfolk.

Instead, Lloyd led the crew of the Seaflower in catching the Spaniards off guard and sailing scot-free to the West Indies.

"Everybody was trying to find a way to get a piece of this treasure — the customs officers, the North Carolina governor and the Outer Bankers — but it was Lloyd who did it," Amrhein says.

"There were no swords drawn, nobody killed, just a very gutsy and daring move by a guy who saw an opportunity to get even."

What Lloyd and his shipmates did next singles them out just

as much as the audacity of their heist and the scale of their haul.

Intent on coming into port without arousing suspicion, they divided and buried their loot, setting the stage for the pirate myth made famous by Robert Louis Stevenson in "Treasure Island."

"Despite what you hear, it's the only case of buried pirate treasure that I've been able to verify," says noted maritime historian Donald G. Shomette, author of numerous histories on pirates and sea raiders.

Just how Stevenson discovered Lloyd's tale some 130 years later isn't known. But there are plenty of circumstances that link it to "Treasure Island."

The author's great-grandfather was a prominent merchant trader on St. Kitts, where Lloyd became a folk hero. His grandfather and father — who were celebrated lighthouse designers — linked him closely to the global sugar and tobacco shipping hub of Glasgow, Scotland, where mariners and newspapers had followed reports of the notorious theft closely.

Still more telling is the 1750 date Stevenson's father provided for the novel's famous map, echoing the year of Lloyd's adventure.

"We know that Stevenson read a lot of early pirate histories," adds Mark G. Hanna, a University of California-San Diego historian who studied colonial piracy at the College of William and Mary's Omohundro Institute of Early American History and Culture.

"But there's no telling what else he heard."

Sadly for Lloyd, there was no storybook ending.

Treasure hunters from across the islands swarmed to unearth his loot, and he died mysteriously in 1752.

"I don't think it ended well," Amrhein says, "because when Lloyd's money ran out, so did the people he was paying for protection."

Mark St. John Erickson   41

Illustrations

English engraver Benjamin Cole created this image of Blackbeard for the 1724 edition of Capt. Charles Johnson's "General History of the Robberies and Murders of the most notorious Pyrates."

Out of the Sea Came Pirates!

Fearing the establishment of a pirate colony on the Outer Banks, Virginia Lt. Gov. Alexander Spotswood secretly organized the Hampton-based Royal Navy expedition that killed Blackbeard at Ocracoke in 1718.

Mark St. John Erickson

43

This illustration from an 1837 book on pirates shows Blackbeard's severed head hanging from the bowsprit as the Royal Navy expedition that killed him in 1718 returned to Hampton.

Out of the Sea Came Pirates!

Blackbeard's crew were likely held in the two original cells of Williamsburg's 1704 Public Gaol.

Mark St. John Erickson

By Gregory Stapko after Sir Peter Leyden/Courtesy of the Jamestown-Yorktown Foundation

Virginia Gov. Sir William Berkeley organized the colony's unsuccessful attempts to resist two Dutch raids on the tobacco fleets in Hampton Roads during the late 1600s.

Out of the Sea Came Pirates!

Dutch artist Willem van de Velde painted this circa 1670 naval scene showing a Dutch warship similar to those used in two late 1600s raids on the
Virginia tobacco fleet in Hampton Roads.

Mark St. John Erickson

Painted in his chest armor while brandishing a pistol, Dutch sea raider Jacob Binckes was co-commander of the fleet of privateers who captured most of the Virginia tobacco fleet from Hampton Roads and the James River in 1673.

Out of the Sea Came Pirates!

Dutch sea raider Cornelis Evertsen — known as "Kees the Devil" — was co-commander of the fleet of privateers who captured most of the Virginia tobacco fleet from Hampton Roads and the James River in 1673.

Mark St. John Erickson

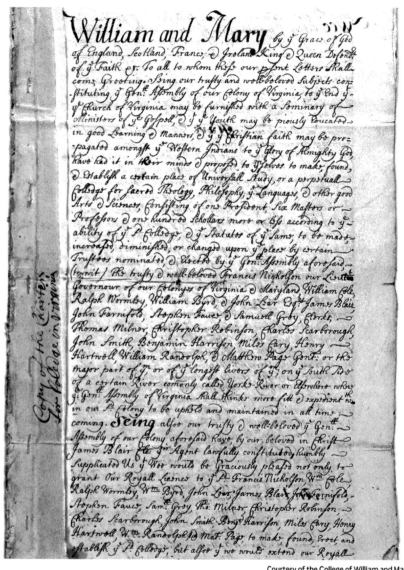

The College of William and Mary received its royal charter in 1693 after three English pirates captured in Hampton Roads and held at Jamestown agreed to donate part of their loot to the school's founder, Rev. James Blair.

Out of the Sea Came Pirates!

Founder Rev. James Blair added significantly to original endowment of the College of William and Mary by arranging to exchange 300 pounds in pirate loot for his assistance in helping three English brigands captured in Virginia regain their freedom and the rest of their plunder.

Mark St. John Erickson

VOYAGE

AND

DESCRIPTION

OF THE

Isthmus of *America,*

Giving an Account of the

AUTHOR's *Abode* there,

The *Form* and *Make* of the *Country*, the *Coasts, Hills, Rivers,* &c. *Woods, Soil, Weather,* &c. *Trees, Fruit, Beasts, Birds, Fish,* &c.

The *Indian Inhabitants*, their Features, Complexion, &c. their Manners, Customs, Employments, Marriages, Feasts, Hunting, Computation, Language, &c.

With Remarkable *Occurrences* in the *South Sea,* and elsewhere.

By *LIONEL WAFER.*

Illustrated with several Copper-Plates.

English pirate Lionel Wafer wrote a best-selling account of his adventures after buying his freedom and recovering most of his loot with a donation to the original endowment of the College of William and Mary.

CAPTAIN WILLIAM DAMPIER

from an Original Picture in the British Museum

English pirate William Dampier was a shipmate of the pirate trio who donated part of their loot to help found the College of William and Mary. Joining the crew in Hampton, he sailed with them to the west coast of South America before leaving for a round-the-world adventure that later helped inspire "Gulliver's Travels" and "Robinson Crusoe."

The College of William and Mary's historic Wren Building was built in part from funds donated by pirates shortly before the school was chartered in 1693.

Out of the Sea Came Pirates!

PETER HEYMAN
COLLECTOR OF CUSTOMS IN
LOWER DISTRICT OF JAMES RIVER
HE WENT IN PURSUIT OF A PYRATE
WHO GREATLY INFESTED THIS COAST
WAS KILLED
YE 29 DAY OF APRIL, 1700

The remains of Hampton Customs Officer Peter Heyman are still buried in the yard of the third St. John's Church, where a headstone commissioned by Gov. Francis Nicholson describes Heyman's bravery and death in a 1700 battle with "pyrates."

Mark St. John Erickson

Left: This drawing is a copy of a painting believed to portray Virginia Gov. Francis Nicholson.
Below: This early 1700s pistol from the collection of The Mariners' Museum shows a weapon similar to that used by Virginia Gov. Francis Nicholson in a 1700 battle with pirates off Lynnhaven Inlet.

Courtesy of The Mariners' Museum

Closeup of the inscription on the headstone commissioned by Gov. Francis Nicholson in the St. John's Church cemetery (also shown on previous page).

Out of the Sea Came Pirates!

Legendary pirate Bartholomew "Black Bart" Roberts is depicted in this engraving from Capt. Charles Johnson's 1724 "General History of the Robberies and Murders of the most notorious Pyrates." Know as the Crimson Pirate, Roberts swore revenge for the arrest, trial and execution of six of his former shipmates in Virginia in 1720 but was killed in battle before he could carry out his threat.

Six pirates were arrested and tried in Hampton in 1720 after paying their tavern bills with hard currency like these Spanish pieces of eight rather than with tobacco.

Courtesy of Colonial Williamsburg

Mark St. John Erickson

Four of the pirates condemned to death in Hampton in 1720 were later hung up in chains after their executions at Urbanna and Gloucester Point.

Out of the Sea Came Pirates!

"Treasure Island: The Untold Story" details the connections between a Hampton merchant captain and the notorious 1750 Act of Piracy that may have inspired Robert Louis Stevenson's famous 1883 adventure novel, "Treasure Island."

Mark St. John Erickson

59

Out of the Sea Came Pirates!

About the Author

Mark St. John Erickson is an award-winning writer at the Daily Press in Newport News, Va., where he's explored the pioneering and remarkably continuous historical importance of Hampton Roads, the lower Chesapeake Bay and the surrounding region for 25 years. He lives with his wife and son near the waterfront in the old colonial port town of Hampton, Va., which survived its many brushes with pirates, British raiders and Confederate incendiaries to become the oldest continuous settlement in English America.

Also from Daily Press Media Group

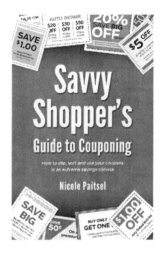

Savvy Shopper's Guide to Couponing

The perfect start for the beginning coupon clipper, the book's easy-to-understand instructions lead novice and veteran couponers alike through the winding maze of saving money at the grocery store. Learn how to organize your coupons, the secrets behind finding the best coupons, and how you can use the drugstores' programs to earn cash.

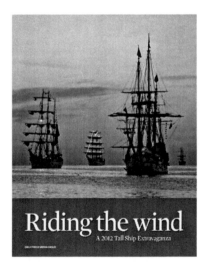

Riding the Wind
A 2012 Tall Ship Extravaganza

OpSail 2012 sailed into Hampton Roads, Va., and Daily Press photographers were there capturing hundreds of moments that reflect the majesty and might of life on the high seas, the best of which are presented here for you to remember and enjoy.

Available now at
www.dailypressstore.com

CPSIA information can be obtained at www.ICGtesting.com
Printed in the USA
BVOW020522171212

308401BV00001B/3/P